Marketing to OCIOs

THE ASSET MANAGER'S GUIDE TO BEING ON
EVERY OCIO SHORT LIST

Russell Campbell

Your Second Opinion, LLC
Las Vegas, Nevada

Your Second Opinion, LLC
7735 Willow Cove Circle
Las Vegas, Nevada 89129
www.yoursecondopinionllc.com
campbell@yoursecondopinionllc.com

Book Layout ©2017 BookDesignTemplates.com

Ordering Information:
Quantity sales. Special discounts are available on quantity purchases by corporations, associations, and others. For details, contact the publisher at the address above.

Marketing to OCIOs/Russell Campbell —1st ed.
ISBN 978-1-7321388-3-4

Contents

To Suzy, thank you for your love and support for so many years

Preface

You probably work for an asset management firm. So you see the opportunities that exist for managing money for outsourced chief investment officer (OCIO) firms. You are aware that these types of firms are growing quickly, and you want a piece of their action. Then you find out that OCIOs are quite different from other kinds of clients.

Few money managers see marketing to this segment as distinct at first glance. Only a few asset managers, for example, have anyone dedicated to OCIO sales as a separate segment, although this is beginning to change.

OCIO sales activities are usually assigned to the same group that sells to investment consultants. But while there is an overlap between consulting and OCIO, not all consultants offer OCIO services.

And even more importantly, not every OCIO firm is also a traditional consultant. Many of these OCIO firms without a consulting history think about investing very differently from the traditional consultant model. They may be asset managers themselves or investment bankers or perhaps managed a large portfolio.

So asset management salespeople may struggle to understand the variety of OCIO flavors, and how to win money management mandates from them.

Describing the landscape is the primary mission of this book. And we'll cover 25 dimensions of that landscape.

Which leads me to my subtitle.

Not all OCIOs have formal short lists. But they all have in mind a way to rank all of the managers and strategies that they choose to consider. This book describes 25 dimensions to consider to put an asset management firm at the forefront of an OCIO's list—formal or otherwise.

I believe that OCIO firms are worth the extra effort to understand. OCIO is already a big part of the industry, and it is growing rapidly. And there is a lot of competition from money managers for OCIO business.

I know that I can help asset managers be prepared to compete and win because of my experience in both the OCIO and asset management worlds.

I've been the CEO of an OCIO firm, consulted to many other OCIO firms on their business and marketing strategies, and advised institutional clients with assets to be managed on the ins and outs of using OCIO firms.

I've also written a book recently, called *OCIO: The Board Members' Guide to Overseeing an Outsourced Chief Investment Officer*.

I think that I have a lot to share about the OCIO world and from multiple perspectives.

Asset managers may think of OCIOs as clients, but the fact is that they are intermediaries who pool the moneys of many clients. This adds to the complexity of marketing to them. Several times in my career, I've also been in an intermediary role, either as an investment consultant or as a manager of managers.

My background also includes asset management. I've been head of marketing at several large money managers and a chief investment officer several times as well.

In addition to drawing on my experiences for this book, I've gathered and analyzed secondary research about OCIO approaches to manager research and selection. I've also spoken to a number of OCIO firms and interviewed asset managers who sell money manager products to OCIOs.

Introduction

"We are all agreed that the client needs an allocation to private equity. But we don't have any products on our approved list that are accepting new allocations. What should we do?"

The members of the investment committee of an OCIO firm were meeting to discuss the portfolio's asset allocation. One of the recommendations from the firm's analysts was to increase the allocation to private equity (PE). The investment committee had several PE managers on their "buy list" to choose from. Unfortunately, all of these firms had recently completed fundraising rounds and were flush with excess cash to invest. None of the preferred PE managers had any interest in accepting additional money at the time.

So the investment committee was stuck. How could they get an allocation to private equity for their clients? What other options did they have?

They could give the money to another unapproved manager—but that didn't make sense.

They could leave the money in cash until their preferred managers were open for business again. But who knew when that would be?

So they picked a third option. The OCIO firm chose to redirect the proposed allocation to private equity into a liquid multi-asset product—a global asset allocation fund.

Huh?

The committee saw the multi-asset product as a short-term substitute for investing in private equity. The OCIO investment committee decided to wait for the next round of fundraising from one of their preferred private equity managers rather than look for another PE manager to add to their buy list.

The multi-asset product shared some characteristics with PE. It offered some equity exposure with limited downside while the investment committee waited for the next PE round.

If you were one of the approved PE managers who declined the money, it would have been a little painful to see this allocation go elsewhere. If you were an unapproved PE manager and had known about this potential allocation to PE, you'd probably have been disappointed that your firm wasn't even considered. On the other hand, if you were the multi-asset manager, you probably would have been thrilled and surprised by this unexpected allocation to your product.

If you are an asset manager, anticipating the needs of OCIO firms may not be as straightforward as it seems.

But first an asset manager needs to be seen as a player—worthy of consideration regardless of the available mandate.

.

CHAPTER 1

Are You a Successful Money Manager?

I have searched for differences between successful and not-so-successful asset managers through multiple research studies that I've conducted. I've identified several characteristics that differentiate the best from the rest. Not coincidentally, OCIO firms also seek these in the managers that they prefer to hire.

Here are four characteristics that are present in the most-successful asset managers.

A robust investment process is one. It's really the only way to improve the odds of realizing future outperformance.

Investment return, or positive alpha in our industry jargon, is an outcome that we all aspire to achieve. OCIO firms are tempted, like most other clients, to pick managers with a great track record. The hope of everyone is that the past is prologue and positive returns will continue into the future.

Unfortunately, many studies have convincingly demonstrated that past returns don't necessarily predict future performance.

But most believe that a credible investment process helps to improve the odds of achieving the alpha goal. So believing in an asset manager's investment process is one way that OCIOs choose a manager with a better chance of meeting their expectations.

Asset managers acknowledge that most professional buyers, including OCIOs, are looking closely at their description of their investment process.

> *"Overwhelmingly, 76 percent of managers cite 'clearly articulating the firm's investment philosophy and process' as an effective way to win new business."—Cerulli*

Next is product focus. Many OCIOs agree that they prefer managers who stick to what they are good at.

> *"Firms that stand out have a clear identity, they know what they are good at, and it is ingrained throughout the firm. The opposite is a firm that is everything to all people, and that says, 'We can do that.'"—Scott Lavelle, PNC*

The fastest-growing asset managers in recent years have fewer, rather than more, products.

Growth in assets under management (AUM) is the third characteristic of successful managers. Growth in AUM signals success to many clients and acts as almost a third-party endorsement of the choice of a manager.

But what drives AUM?

Many asset managers believe that branding helps to drive asset growth. Branding with a capital *"B"* means formal communications in the minds of most people in this industry. And large companies have the biggest budgets to promote their brands formally. There is no doubt that it costs a lot of money to earn brand recognition.

But brand recognition offers no obvious correlation with future growth. I have examined numerous asset manager brand rankings over the years. While a brand ranking tells you where a firm stands today, the rank provides no information about the future growth potential of a firm.

Instead, the best predictor of future growth in AUM that I've discovered is employee satisfaction. *Glassdoor, Indeed, Best Companies to Work For* and similar rankings are useful sources of information on satisfaction. Each service offers relative rankings of firms based on how employees feel about their workplaces.

Based on my research, what employees say to others informally is the most important factor driving asset growth. Here is why. This is a professional service business, and the staff's own word of mouth is highly correlated with future growth in AUM. People talk, and either build or destroy the companies that they represent.

Client service is the fourth main characteristic of successful asset managers. What client service means to OCIO firms is strong communication with their managers.

> *"We want our managers to tell us what is changing in the market, in their strategy, and in their personnel that could affect future performance. We need them to be honest."—Tim Ng, Clearbrook*

Great money managers have a robust investment process that reinforces their historical performance record. They stick to a limited set of products and serve their employees and clients well.

CHAPTER 2

What Do OCIO Firms Promise to Their Clients?

Many money managers feel that their investment offer alone should be enough to win over clients. Some asset managers believe that if they can show great past performance, describe the merits of their investment process, and serve others as well as anyone else does, they should win the business.

But an investment offer isn't enough. Instead, asset managers need to dig deeper into the needs of their prospective clients—in this case by understanding the OCIO's promises to its own clients.

Again, OCIOs are intermediaries. OCIOs may be held responsible for delivering on their promises. And they have to trust that their partners will deliver in tandem with the OCIO.

Asset managers are an essential part of the OCIO's deliverable. If an OCIO promises better investment performance, for example, it will be at least partly as a result of how their money managers perform.

"Because we have ownership of the decision to hire an asset manager, we need high conviction about the managers we hire."—Scott Lavelle, PNC

And it's not only about a promise to deliver on investment performance. OCIOs often make other promises to clients that money managers should be

15

aware of. These promises to the OCIO's clients also affect the relationship between the OCIO and the asset manager.

Typical asset manager-related promises from OCIO vendors include the following:

1. The OCIO firm typically promises to negotiate lower fees from vendors such as asset managers. OCIOs claim that they can reduce the fees paid by clients to money managers because of the combined purchasing power of the OCIO firm's clients. It's true that asset managers will often give a fee break to large clients. But some OCIOs press for further fee discounts. And OCIOs may be tougher than usual negotiators with asset managers. Contract terms—such as guaranteeing access to the asset manager's capacity, or a custom mandate are often negotiated. Money managers have to decide how much capacity to make available, for what capability, and at what price.

2. OCIO firms tell their clients that decisions are made more quickly by the OCIO than by a client. So OCIOs may be quicker to hire and fire than money managers are used to. OCIO firms may also tactically reallocate assets more often. Winning and losing mandates, and abrupt changes in investment flows and outflows, presents both an opportunity and a risk for money managers.

3. Improved investment risk management is another promise often made by OCIOs to their clients. But the efforts made by OCIO firms to manage risk vary a lot, usually based on the resources available to each firm. Whatever the OCIO's process, adjusting the risk taken in client portfolio's may lead to revisions in the terms of an investment mandate or the amount of money allocated to the asset manager.

4. OCIOs promise their clients that the investment portfolio will be more sophisticated. And clients hire them at least partly for that reason. Industry surveys suggest that one of the top reasons for choosing an OCIO is to access a broader range of alternative investments, for instance. So an asset manager's product complexity may be attractive to many OCIOs. However, not all OCIOs are the same. Not all are so enamored with complexity.

"We aren't different for the sake of being different ... This differs from most industry participants that seek to complicate portfolios for sake of complication."—Summit Strategies

Understand and support the OCIO's promises to its clients.

CHAPTER 3

Whom Do They Serve?

"We have the privilege of working with foundations, endowments, and families, and this clientele drives manager research and selection. Our specific client base allows us to focus only on the type of investment managers that are suitable for our clients."—Canterbury Consulting

OCIOs may specialize in serving certain types of clients. While most clients have broadly similar needs (more return!), there will be other differences.

Asset managers may be familiar with the types of clients that a particular OCIO serves. That shared understanding can be helpful to the relationship between the asset manager and the OCIO as both pursue clients. These may include clients as varied as family offices, endowments, foundations, high net worth, defined benefit pension plans, defined contribution plans, Taft-Hartley, or others.

Asset managers may be able to help the OCIO to solve the specific kinds of problems encountered by different types of clients.

For example, some clients need to match their liabilities as closely as possible. Many asset managers can offer liability-driven investing capabilities to an OCIO.

Other clients may be aggressively return seeking. They may be eager to take a chance on a new opportunity—a new manager, an emerging manager, or a new product.

Having a shared understanding of the needs of the OCIO's clients can help to deepen an asset manager's relationship with an OCIO. Understanding the needs of the OCIO and their clients also helps to tailor the asset manager's investment, marketing, and operational advice.

> *"We do not think it is always appropriate to invest in off-the-shelf products ... we look to partner ... to create solutions that meet the specific requirements of our client base."—Willis Towers Watson*

The needs of an OCIO may be quite specific. They might include, for instance, mission-based investing approaches such as ESG, high income, or many other alternative strategies.

> *"We have a dedicated [manager research] MRI team ... [including] ESG, impact and sustainability."—Cambridge*

Tap into your knowledge of the client segments that the OCIO serves, and offer the specific support that may be needed.

CHAPTER 4

What Are They Good At?

One particular OCIO firm hardly markets their services at all. Their prospective clients almost have to beg for discretionary management! After being hired, this firm provides very good operating support to their clients. So this firm has some strengths, including the trust of its clients. But this OCIO risks losing clients in the future because they don't have a competitive investment capability.

An asset manager marketing to this client might choose to first emphasize their back-office support skills to mirror and support the OCIO's own current strengths.

Over time, an asset manager might then try to deepen the partnership with this OCIO by discussing risk management, tactical asset allocation, product selection considerations, trading, and so on.

Other OCIO firms may have different strengths that an asset manager could consider supporting. An OCIO might be a capable asset manager or a fabulous marketing machine, for example. By matching an OCIO's primary expertise and an asset manager's own skills, a custom sales approach can win and keep more business.

Asset managers should reflect on their experience working with any other OCIOs that have hired them already. Why were they hired by these firms? Perhaps an asset manager was hired for their ability to support the OCIO's business needs—not just investment needs. This characteristic may also be valued and sought after by other OCIO firms.

Know the OCIO's main strengths—such as investments, marketing, and/or operations/client service—and support their strengths and weaknesses.

CHAPTER 5

Helping Them beyond Investing

Marketing is often a weak point for many OCIOs. That shouldn't be surprising since most OCIOs have been around for a relatively short period of time and have a lot to learn. Unfortunately for them, the competition is getting tougher by the day, as more firms enter the OCIO business.

Most prospective clients of OCIOs only consider a very short list of OCIO candidates. That is mainly because clients have heard of very few of the firms. So OCIOs have an uphill battle for recognition.

But even when prospective clients are open to considering more OCIOs, it doesn't make an OCIO's sales efforts any easier. Clients who want to look at more options issue RFIs and RFPs to narrow the list of candidates.

Then OCIOs have a new battle to fight. In addition to creating awareness of their services, they also have to differentiate their services from other OCIO's.

Bottom line, OCIO firms have to market themselves. And most could use help.

But some OCIOs—mainly those with a money management heritage—have an advantage. Money managers know how to market with every tool in their toolbox.

For example, the ASU Foundation for A New American University hired BlackRock in 2017 for several reasons, including "a broad partnership to engage in programming and mentorship for ASU undergraduates." This promise from BlackRock goes well beyond typical service offerings.

For those OCIOs without a deep marketing toolkit, the challenge is steep.

But money managers who are marketing to OCIOs can help. Their marketing wisdom has been accumulated over time with many of the same types of clients that OCIOs now face. Money managers can help OCIO firms with their marketing and make that a valuable part of their offer to OCIOs.

OCIO firms may welcome the help. And some lesser-known OCIO firms may also be happy to associate their brands with highly respected asset managers.

OCIOs aren't usually great marketers. Asset managers can help.

CHAPTER 6

What Do They Prefer?

OCIOs make choices about how they approach the investing challenge. Some choose to use only passive investment products. This limits opportunities for active managers to be hired by these firms. But the good news is that entirely passively managed OCIOs are the exception.

> *"If you look at OCIO versus advisory portfolios, you will see more active managers."—AON, eVestment interview*

And even OCIOs that rely mainly on passive investing may include actively managed products in their programs.

> *"Our multi-boutique model is well positioned to offer specialist active and passive solutions."—BNY Mellon*

There are lots of active asset management opportunities in the OCIO world. But how active managers fit into each OCIO's program varies.

Some OCIOs use a simple structure with a few active core managers. As a result, they may have portfolios with less manager turnover, straightforward investment mandates with each manager, and longer-term partnerships with the managers they use.

> *"We want managers that are focused, distinctive, preferably with only one product—with all of their eggs in one basket."—A well-known OCIO firm*

"We don't 'boil the ocean' by having excessive manager turnover."—Clearbrook

Other OCIOs hire numerous specialists within each asset class, which means more specialty opportunities for asset managers.

The downside is that it likely also means higher turnover of managers. Asset managers need to weigh the benefit of associating with an OCIO that has a higher propensity to hire and fire frequently. A more precarious relationship affects the economics of that relationship. There is also the potential for a negative impact on the asset manager's brand if they are fired.

Active versus passive, and the number of active manager strategies used are two of the choices made by OCIOs. But there are other investment decisions made by each OCIO.

In recent years, portfolio risk management considerations have also begun to influence manager selection.

Some OCIOs pay attention to return/risk factors that transcend asset classes. These OCIOs might consider the portfolio's overall exposure to global equities, interest rates, inflation, currencies, and so on. The portfolio's exposure to each of these factors can influence the selection of managers, the strategies selected, and the allocation of money to each manager. And OCIOs want to be convinced that the asset managers they choose understand where they fit into the OCIO's portfolio.

"The price of admission used to be 'We know our positions better than anybody else.' ... That's not best-in-class anymore ... Knowing their interactions, their correlations, the currency effects and exposures, the factor overlaps."—Wells Fargo, quoted in Citywire

So it's not just about investment returns. An OCIO may be interested in how a money manager might diversify the portfolio and contribute to hedging against unexpected events.

Bottom line, the contribution to risk as well as return of a manager and the asset classes that they invest in is of interest to the OCIO.

"For all strategies, fit within the portfolio is extremely important. Fit includes confidence in the asset class, its contribution to diversification, and in the manager's ability to achieve alpha expectations."—SEI

Liquidity is another issue of interest. Some OCIOs are concerned with the overall liquidity of the portfolio. This may simply be a desire to be prepared for day-to-day liquidity to meet withdrawals, or to allow for additions to the portfolio from new contributions and new clients.

Or their concern about liquidity may be deeper. The OCIO may want to be prepared for occasions when a bear market hits, or underperformance occurs, and clients demand their money back sooner than expected. If an asset manager's products offer more liquidity than competitors', without sacrificing return, this can be an advantage in marketing and winning OCIO mandates.

Include a discussion of big picture issues in your offer, such as a product's exposure to factors (equities, rates, inflation, currencies, or diversification and hedging), contribution to portfolio risk, or portfolio liquidity.

Fighting the Passive Monster

If it's straight-up index funds that the OCIO firm prefers, it's probably not going to be a good day for an active manager to close new business.

But what if there's a crack in this approach? Perhaps they use smart beta approaches, for example.

> *"We always want to avoid paying up for a return stream that we could access in a less expensive way."—Hirtle Callaghan*

Even OCIOs that are known for being mainly passive make room for some active management if they believe it's of benefit. State Street and Vanguard are two of the largest passive managers available, for instance. But both acknowledge that they do use (some) external active managers.

> *"[We] allocate to active managers as a satellite allocation."—State Street Global Advisors*

> *"Contrary to popular belief, active and index investing are not opposing philosophies, but complementary techniques ... [We] can provide access to renowned investment firms ... We are one of the largest buyers of investment management services."—Vanguard*

The list of active managers used by passively oriented OCIO firms is shorter than most other OCIO firms, but the size of mandates is often significantly larger. This makes it worthwhile, especially for larger asset managers, to pursue opportunities with these OCIO firms.

Is there a window available for active management products?

CHAPTER 8

What Do They Expect from Their Active Managers?

"Managers must meet a number of qualitative and quantitative elements."—
Salim Shariff, Aptitude Investments

Every OCIO has its own manager selection criteria. Many of these criteria can be addressed by asset managers in writing and verbally, and most money managers have lots of practice in doing this. Later, we'll discuss a specific approach that may be helpful to asset managers if they have had difficulty in expressing their edge.

The bigger issue may be fitting into the OCIO firm's expectations from a quantitative perspective. Quant analysis of returns and holdings, and especially risk, is what it is. If you don't make the cut, there may be little that you can do beyond offering explanations or context. Relationships can be helpful as well.

There are exceptions made in every manager selection process. The quantitative analysis may not tell the whole story, and asset managers should be prepared to provide the fuller story.

There are exceptions to the rule in every manager selection process.

CHAPTER 9

Do They Do it Themselves?

Most OCIOs outsource active investment management to others.

> *"With no manager relationships or internal products of any kind, we can be truly objective in identifying best-in-class managers."—Meketa*

But there are other OCIO firms that hang on tight to some mandates, and they do not outsource.

This cuts the opportunity set for active managers.

> *"In situations where SSGA has dominant investment capabilities, we will use them inside client portfolios. Otherwise we will use external managers. Client contracts stipulate the maximum allocation to internal managers."—State Street*

Active expertise may be offered through the OCIO's internal investment management or even via ownership positions in actively managed firms that are owned by the OCIO firm.

Is there ANY room for any external managers?

CHAPTER 10

Is Their Business in Jeopardy?

Is it even worthwhile to pursue every OCIO? An asset manager may choose to ignore some of these firms as prospects.

First, be wary of OCIO firms with limited resources. An OCIO will struggle to compete in the long run if they lack adequate resources—people, technology, and so on. Clients typically want their OCIOs to consider every investment possibility. OCIOs have to have substantial resources to be able to consider the entire world of investment options. If they lack the resources, they may retain some clients for a while, but the odds of survival are against them. Eventually, clients will discover that there are better-resourced, more stable and capable OCIO firms available. Money managers should be able to recognize whether an OCIO has the horsepower to do the job for the long run.

Second, poor investment performance could also be a caution sign for asset managers who are considering partnering with an OCIO. The problem for asset managers is that OCIO performance is not public information, so it's not easy to figure out who is doing well and who isn't. But there is an industry grapevine, and there are ways to triangulate how a particular OCIO is performing. Client losses, public-domain documents from clients who are legally obliged to disclose information, reports on performance from industry surveys, and media reports can all provide clues as to the investment performance of an OCIO firm. While short-term performance varies, as we all well know, asset managers should be sensitive to any structural problems that may be limiting an OCIO's ability to deliver to clients.

Third, investment staff turnover is a warning sign. Money managers are acutely aware of how turnover of their own senior investment officers can put them in the penalty box or on watch lists. For now, most OCIO firms downplay the impact of any turnover because they are not being held accountable for investment staff turnover by their clients. But if CIOs and senior investment people leave an OCIO firm, asset managers may want to be a little more cautious about working with a particular OCIO. Investment performance may be better or worse in the future, but clients may be unhappy later with personnel changes now or even become very unhappy if results decline.

Fourth, what's worse than personnel turnover? How about incompetence! As Warren Buffett once said, "Only when the tide goes out do you discover who's been swimming naked." Some OCIOs lack hands-on money management experience. In the short run, skill is hard to judge, but asset managers may be able to anticipate issues that may appear in the longer run.

Let me exaggerate for a moment to make a point.

Anyone can allocate money into a 60 percent equity/40 percent fixed-income portfolio, implement this policy with a selection of brand-name money managers, and then rebalance back to 60/40 every quarter.

If it were this easy to manage a portfolio, everyone would do it. Unfortunately, there are people who think that managing money is this easy!

The day of reckoning will come, and some of these pretenders will cause considerable client suffering. A static allocation, hiring the list of currently top-performing money managers, and rebalancing isn't going to lead to long-term success. So asset managers may want to be cautious about being a part of these naïve programs.

Finally, there are long-term threats to some OCIOs. Conflicts of interest are rampant in the business—only some of which are recognized. While most OCIOs are regulated, there have been surprisingly few enforcement actions for misbehavior from regulators.

Asset managers are more sensitive than many OCIOs to the risks of regulatory punishment. They have lived through increasing regulation in recent years. Asset managers should have a sixth sense about which OCIO firms are at risk of feeling a regulator's wrath. We'll look at some of these risks next.

Be cautious if an OCIO appears to be struggling. Consider the impact on an asset manager's brand.

CHAPTER 11

What to Watch Out For

There are many ways that OCIO firms could get into trouble with regulators. Just ask the compliance departments of any asset management firm. OCIOs are supposed to adhere to the same regulations as asset managers, for the most part. But most OCIOs are much less cognizant of regulatory risks. And for now, regulators have been relatively kind to OCIOs. But this could change.

Vendors to OCIOs should try to be sensitive to any risky practices at OCIOs. Here are just a few examples:

1. Failing to disclose potential conflicts of interest to clients
2. Improper accounting
3. Favoring certain clients over others, for example, when allocating capacity to capacity-constrained vehicles or capabilities
4. Making errors or giving incomplete data to clients
5. Steering clients toward more-profitable products or services
6. Not adhering to professional standards

Money managers have experience in working with regulators. OCIOs are less familiar.

CHAPTER 12

What Are Clients Thinking?

Regulators aren't the only ones, of course, who are scrutinizing OCIOs. OCIO clients are becoming more demanding. That's because many clients have lived with OCIOs for some time and have acquired a deeper understanding of what OCIO firms can deliver and what a client should expect.

But it's still difficult for clients to find out everything that they want to know. Consider performance and fees, for instance.

1. No surprise, investment performance varies between OCIO firms. But as mentioned earlier, investment performance in this industry is not transparent. And so the clients of OCIOs can't be sure if their OCIO is any better or worse than the rest. Clients might muse, for example, "Maybe our performance is worse than others because our unique needs require a different, perhaps less-aggressive and therefore lower-expected-return portfolio."
2. Fees charged by OCIOs have declined in recent years. Here too, there is a lack of transparency. Unless a client is searching for a new provider, it's hard for them to know if they could obtain the same or better OCIO services more cheaply—even from their current provider!

Someday we'll be able to make direct comparisons of performance and fees between OCIO vendors. For now, asset managers should be aware of the lack of transparency that exists in the OCIO space, though some are a little less opaque than others.

The clients of OCIOs have their own challenges in working with an OCIO. Investment performance and fees are examples of two important issues that are difficult to compare to others.

CHAPTER 13

Is the Firm Speeding Ahead?

It's tough to figure out who is winning and who is losing market share in the OCIO business. Several sources offer survey data on the level of OCIO AUM. How these lists are compiled, and the resulting accuracy, is a question mark in my view. Firms vary in how they report discretionary versus nondiscretionary AUM, for example.

Some regulatory filings include discretionary and nondiscretionary assets for OCIOs. But even if a survey reports the data accurately or a regulatory filing is available, the information is unhelpful for forecasting the future growth potential of an OCIO.

Asset managers need predictive tools in order to be able to market efficiently. For instance, an asset manager may prefer to partner with OCIOs that are growing more quickly than the rest. An asset manager can win business by replacing existing managers that are being used by OCIOs, but why not target the fast growers first?

A growing OCIO is a terrific distribution channel for a money manager. This channel provides access to clients who may never be available to the money manager.

But how can an asset manager guage the likelihood of an OCIO's future growth?

Some people say that the best OCIO brands will be the winners—just like in asset management. The problem is that there isn't any evidence that the best brands at a point in time also continue to be the future winners. There just isn't any evidence of a correlation between current brand reputation and future growth. As I mentioned earlier, the firm's brand tells you about today's popularity, not tomorrow's success.

So how else can we predict the path of future growth of an OCIO prospect?

I have done a number of studies on what drives growth in assets under management for asset managers. Employee satisfaction is one very useful measure. Employee satisfaction seems to be one of the root causes of rapid growth in asset management, including OCIOs. Maybe it's because satisfied employees in these professional service organizations stay with their firms, are happy with their employer, and tell everyone of their great experience. Happy employees send positive messages out to the world.

Happy employees tell everyone about their experience. Or at least they aren't grumbling about their work and sending negative vibrations into the atmosphere. When intermediaries and clients hear bad things through the grapevine, often spread initially by employees of the firm itself, they lose confidence in the firm. The bottom line is that firms with positive word of mouth grow faster than others, and the firms with negative word of mouth shrink.

OCIO firms have similar results to asset managers. Once again, OCIOs that score highly with their employees grow assets more quickly than their competitors.

In one study, I looked at the 48 OCIO firms with employee ratings on Glassdoor. Of these 48 firms, just seven firms scored 4.0 or higher—less than 15 percent of the firms. All of these firms have experienced above-average growth in outsourced assets under management in recent years.

My conclusion is that there is a widening gap between winners and losers in the growth of outsourced assets. And one strong indicator of this widening gap is evident when you look at employee satisfaction.

Winners are doing a better job of nurturing employee satisfaction. Paying attention to the satisfaction of the employees of OCIOs is helpful to asset managers in choosing which OCIO firms to spend their marketing dollars on.

We are in a professional service business. If employees hate working at an OCIO firm and their views leak out, the firm is doomed. On the other hand, when employees brag to others about their firm's leadership, career opportunities, compensation and benefits, collegiality, and so on, it means that they are satisfied, engaged, and excited, and feel like they are part of a winner. Those feelings are contagious, they spread to the wider community, and they directly lead to growth in AUM.

Investigate whether the OCIO's employees speak highly or poorly of their employer. Their views are predictive of growth.

CHAPTER 14

Are They Active in Other Countries?

What do you know about an OCIO's nondomestic business? Are there differences in the investment strategies that they use elsewhere to accommodate local preferences? There may even be different types of clients served by an OCIO in other markets.

Asset managers need to understand the opportunity with OCIOs that are active abroad. They should ask questions, do some research, and be prepared to customize their approach. As a part of this research into the OCIO's foreign activities, consider whom the OCIO competes with. Is the OCIO firm beating their competition in other markets?

Many asset managers may be familiar with other markets through direct selling or distribution. An asset manager may have experience in marketing in foreign markets that can also be offered to an OCIO to help them to succeed.

If an OCIO operates elsewhere, consider the OCIO's local investment strategies, clients, and competitors.

CHAPTER 15

How Can You Break In?

Growth opportunities for active managers are limited. Most asset managers acknowledge the difficulties they face. I recently conducted a survey of CFOs of major asset managers and asked them how they were most likely to grow their business. Over 90 percent of the survey participants said that taking business away from competitors represented their firm's main opportunity for growth.

OCIO is a notable exception. While there is manager turnover in this space as well, the overall amount of assets managed by OCIOs is growing quickly.

Growth in the OCIO business is a result of a rethinking of asset allocation and how to mix and match asset manager mandates.

But asset managers still have to compete for these opportunities. This growth opportunity isn't available to everyone. The good news is that the breadth of mandates available to be won has grown considerably.

OCIOs with a consulting heritage may be most familiar to asset managers and so, easy to work with. Asset managers know that investment consultants monitor thousands of managers and products, and a few selections end up on the consultant's approved-to-buy list.

Further good news is that consultant-driven OCIOs seem to use a broad selection of products from their buy lists.

Relationships matter a lot when selling to consultants in the nondiscretionary consulting business. And there is carryover in these relationships to the

OCIOs that have emerged from consulting firms. So money managers are comfortable pursuing these OCIO opportunities, and they are pretty happy with the results. Money managers report greater success at winning OCIO mandates from traditional consulting businesses than from other types of OCIOs, according to Cerulli.

But not all OCIOs have a consulting heritage. Marketing to other kinds of OCIOs has different challenges. Asset managers have to ask more questions—and sometimes settle for fewer answers. The OCIO may not signal why they hire the managers they do, what minimum standards they require, and whom they won't touch.

OCIO firms without a consulting heritage often think somewhat differently about how they invest. They may have fewer research resources—by choice or simply because they have less AUM to manage.

The good news is that OCIOs with a different heritage—investment bankers, asset owners, or money managers—may seek longer-term partnerships, and they may be more open-minded.

> *"We will consider a track record for a strategy even if from a previous firm."*—
> Scott Lavelle PNC

OCIOs that have emerged from nondiscretionary consulting firms may operate differently than other OCIOs.

CHAPTER 16

Whom Do You Have to Beat?

Asset managers can easily find information about their competitors. Morningstar, eVestment, and many other databases are great resources.

But OCIOs are not necessarily as enamored with, or dependent on, the ubiquitous databases.

> *"We do not rely on manager database products as we do not believe that these generic resources provide good and actionable information."—Morgan Creek*

> *"Our research teams are very experienced, [and this] allows us to go well beyond the standard 'check the box' approach to manager selection."—Meketa Investment Group*

If the manager relies too heavily on databases to do their marketing for them, they may miss out on opportunities.

There aren't so many OCIO firms to talk to. Money managers need to reach out directly more.

Asset managers should also look to provide additional value—added to their prospective OCIO customers. Whitepapers and other useful investment insights may be valued by OCIO firms. OCIOs may also prefer firms that enable a seamless operating environment. Last, relationships matter too. Your OCIO has to trust that you will be a strong partner.

> *"The manager must have respect for low-probability, known and unknown events. The manager doesn't necessarily have to hedge against these risks, but they should know how they will react."—Salim Shariff, Aptitude*

Have a competitive advantage that is meaningful to each OCIO.

CHAPTER 17

What Triggers an Opportunity for You?

An OCIO may decide to replace a manager for a variety of reasons. Poor performance and changes in the organization or investment process are common reasons.

One OCIO firm hired a money manager who appeared to have a consistent investment process. However, after a lengthy period of underperformance, the investments owned in the manager's portfolio suddenly looked very different. The manager attempted to explain that there was no inconsistency in their approach. The OCIO was suspicious. The OCIO concluded that the manager had gotten fed up with underperforming and, as a result, had made a drastic shift in their investment process. The OCIO terminated the manager because of the changes in process, not simply because of poor performance.

Manager changes may also be for portfolio-related reasons.

There may be a shuffle in the total number of managers used either within or across asset classes. This turnover may illuminate a change in preference of the OCIO for different types of managers. Existing managers may be eliminated, mandates may be altered, or additional managers may be hired.

Another reason for a manager change is because an OCIO has a fundamentally different approach to manager selection. An OCIO firm may explicitly reject the conventional approach of buying managers high and selling them low. Instead, they may try to hire managers when they are out of favor, for style reasons. They then dump the ones who are doing well simply because the manager has caught the wave that favors their investment style. So managers may be replaced because they are doing too well!

Similarly, if the asset class or style is outperforming, an OCIO may choose to rebalance the portfolio because they anticipate a change in prospective returns.

> *"Successful manager selection is not solely dependent upon manager skill, but also on the level of opportunity that exists within the area in which the manager seeks excess returns."—SEI*

Manager turnover presents new opportunities.

CHAPTER 18

Who Looks at Your Material First?

Asset managers who are just starting to pursue OCIO business might want to be more selective at first. An asset manager might consider pursuing small to medium-sized OCIOs with a consulting heritage, for example. Even newer asset managers are generally familiar with how consulting firms think. These consulting firms typically use similar manager selection disciplines for their OCIO business.

Smaller consulting firms also have fewer analysts, and often have centralized decision making for the OCIO part of their business. Having fewer key people allows an asset manager the opportunity to develop personal relationships. That's important when there isn't a "buy list" or an "approved list" of managers.

> *"We do not rely on a roster of favorite, or preferred, managers. Instead each search is conducted in an open, competitive manner."—Meketa Investment Group*

In every case, an asset manager's product description will land on the desk of an analyst at an OCIO for their review. Then the analyst makes a recommendation to more senior personnel or a committee. These investment analysts vary in their experience, quality, and judgment. And there's no correlation between these three characteristics.

If an asset manager has any knowledge of or influence over the inner workings of the OCIO, they should try to steer the analysis of the asset management firm to an analyst or decision maker who is highly regarded internally. Some analysts are more respected than others in any firm, and it can be helpful to have this analyst on the asset manager's side.

Know the gatekeeper's needs, people, and process

CHAPTER 19

Who Are the Deciders?

The deciders may be a committee or an individual. There may be several tiers of decision making in some firms. Asset managers should know these tiers, the decision makers, and their preferences.

I've been on the inside of these decisions. Worst case, even a positive recommendation from a researcher may be ignored. The analyst report may go straight into a file. The decision maker may have already decided who they want to manage a particular sleeve in the portfolio. This happens less frequently than it used to—or so I'm told. Regardless, relationships still matter.

If it's a larger firm, there may be a multi-stage review process.

> "The Investment Manager Oversight Team, comprised of senior investment leaders, oversee the manager due diligence process and procedures. The IMOT is responsible for overseeing the analysis and approving recommendations from the Manager Research Team."—State Street Global Advisors

Any decision-making process may have further guardrails around it as well. Decisions may be made by committee but subject to a process that is enshrined in a policy.

> "It is NEPC's policy that only Focused Placement List managers can be hired into a discretionary portfolio."—NEPC

Not all OCIOs have one CIO, one or more committees, or even one set of analysts. Some have multiple separate decision makers, often distinguished by the types of clients they serve. There may be a CIO who leads the endowment practice, for example. They may have the authority to select different managers or products that they believe fit best with their particular set of clients.

> *"Given that we make customized recommendations to each client ... investment directors may rely on their own research in making recommendations."—Cambridge*

Some firms allow even more customization. They rely on the experience of the OCIO's staff and their personal preferences, and may even create individual solutions for each of their clients.

> *"We follow a generalist consulting approach. Our consultants conduct manager research using their experience with support from analysts."—Ellwood*

Bottom line, regardless of the decision-making process, the OCIO has to believe that an asset manager is the best in class or at least the best fit for their portfolio.

Know the decision makers and their processes

CHAPTER 20

Who Are the Influencers?

In nearly all OCIO firms, those with influence over the manager selection process include investment research and portfolio management staff, which we have already discussed.

There is also usually an operational and compliance element to the due diligence. There are good reasons for OCIOs to care about an asset manager's operations.

> *"A recent study of over 300 hedge fund failures showed that the leading causes of operational failure were theft and misappropriation, followed by misleading existence of assets, legal and regulatory violations, concealment of trading losses, and marketing misrepresentation. As a result, this has painfully reminded institutional investors (and regulators) of the critical need to properly evaluate a fund's legal and operational infrastructure prior to investing, and then on an ongoing basis."—Greenwich Roundtable*

The number of operational failures that have occurred may be surprising to many people. We usually remember the spectacular investment performance-related fund failures. But operations failures are also a big problem. And OCIOs would prefer to avoid them.

The OCIO model is built to provide significant client operating support. The clients of OCIOs expect their provider to monitor compliance and keep the assets and reputation of the client safe.

> *"Manager integrity, strong operational controls, proper incentives, and safety of assets must be beyond all question for us to consider a manager."*—Hirtle Callaghan

And everything is on the table. Operational due diligence can be comprehensive and in considerable depth.

> *"Operational due diligence [includes] infrastructure and resources, governance, policies and procedures, compliance, legal."*—State Street

On an ongoing basis, OCIO firms also watch to see that the manager is living up to expectations as well.

> *"We find an average of eight investment manager purchase/holdings violations per week."*—Investment Performance Services

Investment expertise is not sufficient.

CHAPTER 21

Pitching to Close Business

There are many attributes that are considered by OCIO firms in making their manager selections. Asset managers know the importance of their pitch and work hard to deliver a great one. However, while asset managers may recognize the challenge, they still aren't great at delivering the info that clients of OCIOs want. The preeminent database provider says,

> *"The number-one complaint that we hear from investors and consultants is that managers do a poor job differentiating themselves."—eVestment*

So let's discuss how an asset manager can more clearly convey a philosophy and process. We'll make this a very practical discussion of how to win over an OCIO.

I've seen (and delivered) a lot of presentations. I've been a consultant, a manager of managers, CIO, head of marketing, and head of an OCIO firm. So I can offer my 40 years of experience in listening to pitches.

But my experience doesn't make me unique. There are many people who have seen a lot, and they all think they know what makes a good pitch. So I need to suggest something more.

I've seen—and I still remember—the presentations that were stunning! When there was a client present, they signed up immediately.

So let's start there. What was so special about the content of those presentations that wowed me and other people?

I developed a hypothesis about what makes a great presentation that has four parts to it. I then tested my hypothesis by reviewing what third-party manager research teams said about the top-selling money manager products of recent years. What I found is that the top-selling products include each of the four parts in their pitches.

The first part of a great presentation is defining what you do. What category are you in? The OCIO has to be able to understand where an asset manager's product fits into their portfolio. Seems obvious—but sometimes it isn't. I began this book with an example of the use of a product being used for an unexpected purpose: a multi-asset/global allocation product that was used in place of private equity.

Asset managers need to consider where their product fits for an OCIO's needs right now.

And it might not be strictly an investment question. Your product may fit into another category entirely.

> *"In multi-manager services you will find ... emerging and minority manager program."—Northern Trust*

The second part of a great presentation should prove to the OCIO that the asset manager is "smart." For example, a value-oriented equity asset manager might say, "We have a model that averages the results from multiple valuation techniques." This answer begins to define who the firm is, starts to distinguish the manager from other firms with a similar approach, and helps to draw the OCIO closer to understanding the asset manager's distinctiveness.

The third part of a great presentation is showing what makes the asset manager not only smart but also "clever." For example, a bond money manager might say, "We calculate internal credit scores to establish a fair yield spread, and then adjust our calculated fair yield premium for illiquidity and potential event risk." The cleverness should help to draw clients even deeper into the manager's world, hopefully making the OCIO say "Wow." Ideally, you want the OCIO to acknowledge that not only can the OCIO not do this themselves, but they probably don't know anyone else who can do it either.

The first three parts of a presentation are a little assertive, maybe even "pushy." The asset manager is trying to convince the OCIO that they are both smart and clever.

Now it's time for some humility and self-awareness.

The fourth part of the pitch should round out the discussion. The OCIO firm's analyst may be wondering about the downside of hiring a firm that presents itself as smart and clever. Arrogance and the potential for future disasters may come to mind.

"Managers have to lack hubris."—Salim Shariff, Aptitude

So it is essential for the asset manager to show the OCIO what is being done to mitigate the risks of a manager's approach. For example, a money manager might say, "We have created customized risk dashboards."

The point is to demonstrate that the manager is not only smart and clever but also not so arrogant and that helps to build trust. An asset manager doesn't want an OCIO to be worrying that things might go awry unexpectedly.

"Style drift is a common problem, and it results in the unintended risk exposures that may be outside the client's intended risk budget."—Verus

There are many people who believe that they are experts in winning business by presenting content effectively. This four-part approach is my contribution to this discussion, based on the best presentations I've seen in 40 years in business.

Where do you fit, how is your approach both smart and clever, and how do you mitigate the risks of your approach? Third-party research confirms that these four parts are consistent with the buying criteria of money manager research teams for the top-selling active money manager products in recent years.

A great presentation describes fit, how the product is both smart and clever, and how risk is managed

CHAPTER 22

Are Changes Presenting Fresh Opportunities?

Asset managers need to watch for turnover in the people working at the OCIOs that they are targeting. Changes in personnel at OCIOs appear to happen more often than in asset management generally. Turnover may be in analyst coverage or the decision makers. If there has been significant turnover, this can be an opportunity for an asset manager who is trying to break in.

"Going back to the well" may not feel like the right thing to do. An asset manager may have knocked on the OCIO's door so many times that their knuckles bleed. The manager may have swamped email boxes with glowing investment performance results for years and been ignored. Asset managers may have nearly given up trying.

But changes in people often sweep in fresh thinking, and an asset manager's capability may be just right for the new regime in charge at the OCIO firm.

Major personnel moves are often highlighted in the media, but money managers should stay alert to turnover in other personnel as well. Pay attention if former contacts have left the firm.

Welcome OCIO people turnover. Refresh the offer and go back in.

CHAPTER 23

Custom Mandates or Not

Successful money managers are usually careful about allowing too many clients to have custom versions of their capabilities. And some OCIOs prefer that they keep it simple.

> *"We prefer managers who recognize their limitations and stick to their core competency."—Hirtle Callaghan*

But other OCIOs have very complex investment programs, and they are looking for something special. They may not want plain-vanilla products regardless of how great the investment returns have been. The OCIO may want to have unique products which can then be combined to serve specific purposes. So they ask for atypical mandates.

> *"We look to partner with you [the asset manager] to create solutions that meet the specific requirements of our client base ... [with] an explicit goal of improving diversity, removing redundancy, and best complementing current portfolios."—Willis Towers Watson*

On the one hand, having a set of customized investment product orphans to serve OCIO clients is not healthy for the efficiency or profitability of an asset manager. But money managers may not want to say "no" too quickly to customizing products. The upside of accepting an unusual mandate from an OCIO is that once the mandate is won, the OCIO does most of the marketing, and there is the potential that the OCIO will build scale in the product for the asset manager.

Also, an asset manager may learn something new by agreeing to accept custom mandates. The asset manager may learn about new purposes for their capabilities. This may open doors. For instance, a micro-cap equity mandate may be used by an OCIO as a substitute for private equity.

Be willing and able to consider customizing capabilities.

CHAPTER 24

Case Studies

1. One OCIO has an inexperienced group of investment analysts. They only recommend asset managers who are well known—household names—to their firm's decision makers. In addition, there are several decision makers who make their own decisions for their own set of clients. Asset managers who win mandates from this firm have established personal relationships with these decision makers.

2. Another OCIO firm has a distinct investment style. They combine passive approaches with managers who may be out of favor stylistically but who have strong brands. Managers are invariably surprised when they receive asset flows from the OCIO when the asset manager's performance is in the fourth quartile and they are at risk of losing most of their other clients. However, these same money managers may have money taken away from them by the OCIO when they are performing well. The OCIO takes money away when they believe that the performance is peaking. In addition, both outperforming and underperforming active managers regularly see outflows to more passive strategies, when the OCIO wants to reduce costs and yet still achieve similar expected returns.

3. Another OCIO has both affiliates and in-house expertise. External asset managers will struggle to win against these "internally managed" active products. The OCIO is unlikely to fire staff or divest an ownership position even if an external manager's product is terrific.

4. Some OCIOs have a manager selection process that offers broad latitude to multiple CIOs in the firm who each have responsibility for a select group of clients. It may be possible to approach these CIOs independently

and build relationships which may help to facilitate passing through the usual regular manager selection process.

Every OCIO is unique.

CHAPTER 25

How Are OCIO Firms Likely to Evolve?

There are a number of trends in the OCIO space underway now.

1. Clearly, regulatory guidance will become more intrusive in the future than it is today. There have been very few enforcement actions taken against OCIO firms to date. OCIO firms may be a little complacent now about the likelihood and impact of regulatory actions, but that will change.
2. OCIOs should simplify their investment approaches. Many OCIOs have an overly diversified portfolio. Just as many OCIOs prefer managers who are specialized, clients too may eventually want their OCIOs to keep it simple and relevant to their specific needs.
3. Asset allocation methods will continue to evolve. Quarterly rebalancing to strategic targets will someday be seen as quaint and naïve.
4. Some OCIOs have state-of-the-art risk management—but most do not. Risk management is more important than alpha to many clients.
5. Risk management is not just about reducing risk. OCIOs need to take enough risk in order to meet client goals. For example, investing in equities is risky but ultimately required to beat inflation and grow the size of a long-term portfolio.

6. CIO and vendor fees will continue to be pushed lower over time, which will lead to difficult conversations with asset managers.
7. As OCIO businesses continue to grow to scale up their business, there will be continue to be tension between efficient growth and customization of client portfolios.
8. Clients are increasingly aware of their economic power and will become more activist in their investing.

In the future, OCIOs will continue to professionalize by upgrading compliance, investment risk management, and ability to meet client missions.

CHAPTER 26

Summary and Checklist

1. Great money managers have a robust investment process that reinforces their historical performance record. They stick to a limited set of products and serve their employees and clients well.

2. Understand and support the OCIO's promise to its clients.

3. Tap into your knowledge of the client segments that the OCIO serves, and offer the specific support that may be needed.

4. Know the OCIO's main strengths—such as investments, marketing, and/or operations/client service—and support their strengths and weaknesses.

5. OCIOs aren't usually great marketers. Asset managers can help.

6. Include a discussion of the big picture issues in your offer, such as a product's exposure to factors (equities, rates, inflation, currencies, or diversification and hedging), contribution to portfolio risk, or portfolio liquidity.

7. Is there a window open for active products?

8. There are exceptions to the rule in every manager selection process.

9. Is there any room for external managers?

10. Be cautious if an OCIO appears to be struggling. Consider the impact on an asset manager's brand.

11. Money managers have experience in working with regulators. OCIO firms are less familiar.

12. The clients of OCIOs have their own challenges in working with OCIOs. Investment performance and fees are examples of two important issues that are difficult to compare to others.

13. Investigate whether the OCIO's employees speak highly or poorly of their employer. Their views are predictive of growth.

14. If an OCIO operates elsewhere, consider the OCIO's local investment strategies, clients, and competitors.

15. OCIOs that have emerged from nondiscretionary consulting firms may operate differently than other OCIOs.

16. Have a competitive advantage that is meaningful to each OCIO.

17. Manager turnover presents new opportunity.

18. Know the gatekeeper's needs, people and process.

19. Know the decision makers and their process.

20. Investment expertise is not sufficient.

21. An offer describes fit, how the product is both smart and clever, and how risk is managed.

22. Welcome OCIO people turnover. Refresh your offer and go back in.

23. Be willing and able to consider customizing capabilities.

24. Every OCIO is unique.

25. In the future, OCIOs will continue to professionalize by upgrading compliance, investment risk management, and ability to meet client missions.

ABOUT THE AUTHOR

Russell Campbell is the CEO of Your Second Opinion, LLC, a management consulting firm focused on asset owners with investment portfolios.

Russell has led five investment groups in his career. Prior to establishing his own firm, Russell was the CEO of The Marco Consulting Group, one of the largest institutional investment consulting firms, with a significant CIO outsourcing (OCIO) business. Previously, he was the EVP of Amcore Bank, where he led the wealth management group—one of the 60 largest bank wealth managers in the United States. Earlier, Russell was the president and CEO of ABN AMRO Asset Management Holdings, Inc., which managed $75 billion in assets, as the U.S. investment management affiliate of ABN AMRO Bank. Russell was promoted to this position after having been the CEO of ABN AMRO Asset Management Canada, Inc. He was previously a vice president and partner of Beutel Goodman, Inc., one of Canada's largest investment counseling firms. His first leadership position was as vice president, Bank of Nova Scotia, where he led the investment management of the bank's own large pension fund, and a family office portfolio.

www.ingramcontent.com/pod-product-compliance
Lightning Source LLC
Chambersburg PA
CBHW021915190326
41519CB00008B/783